HARMONIES OF EXC_____

THE WYNTON MARSALIS STORY

WRITTEN BY:

AMANDA GERALDINE

TABLE OF CONTENTS

INTRODUCTION

Wynton Marsalis, a name synonymous with virtuosity in the world of music, was brought into this world on a balmy October 18th in 1961. His place of origin, none other than the pulsating heart of jazz itself, New Orleans, Louisiana. As the sultry notes of jazz wafted through the humid air of this vibrant city, young Wynton Marsalis was destined to become a maestro, a trailblazer in the realms of trumpetry, composition, and musical education.

The Marsalis family was deeply entrenched in the world of music. Wynton, the second of six sons, was born to Dolores Ferdinand Marsalis and Ellis Marsalis Jr., a pianist and music teacher. The very essence of music coursed through his veins, and he was christened after the legendary jazz pianist, Wynton Kelly. The Marsalis family was a musical powerhouse; Branford Marsalis, his older brother, paved his own path in the world of jazz, while Jason Marsalis and Delfeayo Marsalis, his younger siblings, also embraced the harmonious calling of jazz.

Wynton's tryst with the trumpet was a tale as serendipitous as a jazz improvisation. A chance encounter with renowned trumpeters Al Hirt, Miles Davis, and Clark Terry while seated at a table with his father led to a whimsical suggestion by his father - why not hand Wynton a trumpet, too? Al Hirt, with a generous spirit, volunteered to provide the young prodigy with his very first trumpet. At a tender age of six, Wynton Marsalis held in his hands the instrument that would soon become an extension of his soul.

However, it wasn't until the age of twelve that he truly began to hone his craft. His educational journey took him to Benjamin Franklin High School and the New Orleans Center for Creative

Arts, where he was immersed in the world of classical music by day and embraced the jazz idiom at home, under the tutelage of his father.

Marsalis's musical odyssey was diverse, to say the least. He graced the stages of funk bands, marching bands led by the illustrious Danny Barker, and even found himself as the lone black musician in the New Orleans Civic Orchestra. At the age of fourteen, he clinched a music contest that saw him perform Joseph Haydn's trumpet concerto with the New Orleans Philharmonic, leaving audiences spellbound. Just two years later, he ventured into the intricate territory of Bach, delivering a mesmerizing rendition of Brandenburg Concerto No. 2 in F Major.

At seventeen, Wynton Marsalis found himself among the select few, one of the youngest musicians ever admitted to the prestigious Tanglewood Music Center. He stood at the crossroads of his musical journey, with two prominent institutions beckoning him - the Juilliard School and Northwestern University. Fortune favored the former, and thus began his tenure at Juilliard, a decision that would profoundly influence his trajectory in the world of music.

Over the years, Wynton Marsalis's contributions to the world of music have been nothing short of groundbreaking. With nine Grammy Awards adorning his illustrious career, he stands as a testament to the fusion of classical and jazz genres, achieving an unparalleled feat - winning a Grammy in both categories in the same year. Furthermore, his oratorio "Blood on the Fields" etched its name in the annals of history by becoming the first jazz composition to clinch the prestigious Pulitzer Prize for Music.

In the present day, Wynton Marsalis continues to weave his musical magic as the artistic director of

Jazz at Lincoln Center, sharing the enchanting world of jazz with new generations. His story, an embodiment of passion, dedication, and innate talent, serves as an inspiration to aspiring musicians worldwide, a testament to the enduring power of music to captivate hearts and souls.

CAREER

In the late 1970s, Wynton Marsalis made a pivotal decision that would shape the course of his musical destiny. In pursuit of his passion for the trumpet, he embarked on a journey to New York City, where the venerable Juilliard School beckoned. His goal? To obtain a Bachelor of Music in trumpet performance, with dreams of forging a career in the hallowed halls of classical music. Yet, destiny had other plans for this young virtuoso.

Between 1979 and 1981, Marsalis found himself immersed in the vibrant New York music scene. Although he left Juilliard without a degree, his time there was far from unproductive. In 1980, he embarked on a transformative European tour as a member of the legendary Art Blakey big band. His experiences with Blakey, a jazz luminary, and his tenure with The Jazz Messengers from 1980 to 1982, left an indelible mark on Marsalis. It was during this time that he underwent a profound change of heart regarding his career path, transitioning from the world of classical music to the captivating realm of jazz. He often cited the influence of his years spent playing alongside Blakey as a pivotal factor in this pivotal shift.

Marsalis's debut recording with Blakey marked the inception of his storied jazz career. Just a year later, he embarked on a tour with the iconic Herbie Hancock, further solidifying his place in the jazz pantheon. The year 1982 bore witness to another significant milestone as Marsalis signed a contract with Columbia Records, paving the way for his inaugural solo album.

In the same year, he joined forces with his older brother Branford Marsalis, along with the exceptionally talented Kenny Kirkland, Charnett Moffett, and Jeff "Tain" Watts, to establish a quintet that would make waves in the jazz world. However, this lineup underwent changes in 1985 when Branford and Kenny Kirkland departed to collaborate with Sting on recording and touring endeavors. Undaunted, Wynton Marsalis regrouped, forming another quartet, this time featuring the virtuosic Marcus Roberts on piano, Robert Hurst on double bass, and the rhythmic powerhouse of Watts on drums. Over time, this ensemble expanded, welcoming the likes of Wessell Anderson, Wycliffe Gordon, Eric Reed, Herlin Riley, Reginald Veal, and Todd Williams into its fold.

Marsalis's musical journey has been profoundly influenced by an array of luminaries, with a spectrum spanning Duke Ellington, Miles Davis, Harry Sweets Edison, Clark Terry, Dizzy Gillespie, Jelly Roll Morton, Charlie Parker, Wayne Shorter, Thelonious Monk, Cootie Williams, Ray Nance, Maurice André, and Adolph Hofner. The tapestry of his influences is rich and diverse, reflecting the vast expanse of the jazz landscape.

Beyond his musical prowess, Wynton Marsalis has carved a unique niche for himself as a lecturer and musical ambassador. He has traversed the globe, sharing his knowledge and talent on every continent except the icy confines of Antarctica. His commitment to spreading the magic of jazz and music education is a testament to his enduring passion and dedication, leaving an indelible mark on the world of music.

JAZZ AT LINCOLN CENTER

In 1987, Wynton Marsalis embarked on a journey that would redefine the landscape of jazz music in New York City. He played a pivotal role in inaugurating the Classical Jazz summer concert series at the prestigious Lincoln Center, an institution renowned for its commitment to the arts. This endeavor, born from Marsalis's passion and vision, resonated with audiences and artists alike, marking a significant milestone in the fusion of classical and jazz genres.

The resounding success of the Classical Jazz summer concert series set in motion a remarkable transformation. Jazz at Lincoln Center emerged as a new department within the hallowed halls of Lincoln Center, an acknowledgment of its growing influence and significance. Yet, this was just the beginning of a remarkable evolution.

By 1996, Jazz at Lincoln Center had evolved into an independent entity, standing shoulder to shoulder with illustrious organizations such as the New York Philharmonic and the Metropolitan Opera. At the helm of this dynamic institution stood Wynton Marsalis, assuming the mantle of artistic director. His leadership extended beyond the administrative sphere; he also assumed the role of musical director for the Jazz at Lincoln Center Orchestra, a distinguished ensemble.

The Jazz at Lincoln Center Orchestra found its home at the opulent Rose Hall, a venue that resonated with the soulful strains of jazz. However, its reach extended far beyond the confines of its residence. The orchestra embarked on exhilarating tours, bringing the intoxicating rhythms of jazz to audiences around the world. Education and outreach were paramount, with school visits, radio appearances, television broadcasts, and the production of albums under its label, Blue Engine Records, all serving to enrich the musical tapestry of jazz.

In 2011, Wynton Marsalis orchestrated a remarkable collaboration that reverberated across musical genres. Teaming up with rock legend Eric Clapton, they graced the stage of Jazz at Lincoln Center in a historic concert. This extraordinary performance was not only a testament to the universal language of music but was also immortalized in the form of an album titled "Play the Blues: Live from Jazz at Lincoln Center," an embodiment of the harmonious fusion of jazz and rock.

The story of Jazz at Lincoln Center, under the visionary leadership of Wynton Marsalis, is a testament to the enduring power of music to transcend boundaries and captivate hearts. It stands as a beacon, illuminating the path for jazz enthusiasts and aficionados, ensuring that this quintessential American art form continues to flourish and inspire generations to come.

OTHER WORK

Beyond his illustrious career in music, Wynton Marsalis has left an indelible mark in various other realms, showcasing his versatility and unwavering commitment to the world of arts and education.

In 1986, he ventured into the world of children's television, making charismatic guest appearances on iconic shows such as Sesame Street and Mister Rogers' Neighborhood. These appearances not only entertained but also introduced young minds to the magic of music.

A pivotal moment in his educational outreach came in 1995 when he hosted the enlightening program "Marsalis on Music" on public television. Simultaneously, National Public Radio broadcast his thought-provoking series, "Making the Music." These initiatives were more than just educational;

they were transformative. Both programs were honored with the prestigious George Foster Peabody Award, the pinnacle of recognition in the field of journalism.

In 2005, Marsalis graced the stage of Apple's "It's Showtime" Special Event, where he showcased his musical prowess as the world was introduced to the new iMac with Front Row and the iPod with Video. The synergy between technology and art was further emphasized when Marsalis appeared in an iPod TV advertisement in 2006, featuring his captivating composition "Sparks."

Wynton Marsalis's influence extended into the world of journalism when, in December 2011, he assumed the role of cultural correspondent for CBS This Morning, sharing his insights and expertise on matters of culture and the arts with a broader audience. He also lent his wisdom as a member of the CuriosityStream Advisory Board, contributing to the platform's educational mission.

In the hallowed halls of education, Marsalis held the position of director for the Juilliard Jazz Studies program, nurturing the talents of aspiring jazz musicians. His dedication to education was further exemplified when Cornell University bestowed upon him the title of A.D. White Professor-at-Large in 2015, a role that allowed him to impart his vast knowledge and passion for music to eager minds.

Wynton Marsalis's creative genius extended to collaborations with the Philadelphia Orchestra, where he showcased his prowess as a composer for modern classical music. Notably, the orchestra premiered his Violin Concerto in 2015, followed by his Tuba Concerto in 2021, marking his contributions to the classical repertoire.

In 2019, Marsalis's multifaceted talents found expression in his involvement in the Daniel Pritzker film "Bolden," where he not only composed, arranged, and performed music but also contributed to the sonic tapestry of the cinematic experience.

Wynton Marsalis's journey transcends the boundaries of music, demonstrating how one artist's passion and vision can enrich and elevate the worlds of education, technology, and culture, leaving an indelible legacy for generations to come.

DEBATE ON JAZZ

The realm of jazz, like any art form, is not without its share of debates and divergent perspectives, and Wynton Marsalis stands at the center of one such discussion.

Marsalis is widely recognized as a torchbearer for what is often termed "straight-ahead jazz." This genre harkens back to the roots of jazz, embracing the traditional instruments and eschewing the electronic and fusion elements that gained prominence in the 1970s and 1980s. In his view, the fundamentals of jazz are rooted in blues, standards, a swinging rhythm, tonality, harmony, craftsmanship, and a profound mastery of the jazz tradition, tracing its origins from New Orleans jazz all the way to the innovations of Ornette Coleman.

However, not all critics are in harmony with Marsalis's perspective. Jazz critic Scott Yanow, for instance, acknowledges Marsalis's undeniable talent but questions his "selective knowledge of jazz history." Yanow suggests that Marsalis's definition of jazz excludes post-1965 avant-garde styles and dismisses 1970s fusion as "barren." He attributes some of these beliefs to the influence of Stanley Crouch, a renowned cultural critic.

Pianist Keith Jarrett, in a candid critique, remarked that Marsalis's music sometimes seemed to imitate the styles of others too closely, likening it to the performance of a high school trumpet player.

However, it's essential to recognize that Marsalis has his champions as well. Bassist Stanley Clarke, for example, acknowledges the criticisms but emphasizes the positive contributions Marsalis has made. He lauds Marsalis for bringing respectability back to jazz and appreciates the energy and vitality he brings to the genre.

A noteworthy encounter between Marsalis and one of his idols, Miles Davis, resulted in an exchange that reflects the tension in the jazz community. Davis quipped, "So here's the police...," highlighting his perception of Marsalis as an enforcer of orthodoxy within the genre. In response, Marsalis expressed his disapproval of Davis's foray into rock and pop music, particularly exemplified by Davis's experimental 1970 album, "Bitches Brew," which Marsalis likened to a betrayal of jazz principles.

Marsalis's stance on other genres is also a subject of debate. He has been critical of rap, characterizing it as "hormone-driven pop music" and asserting that hip-hop reinforces destructive behavior at home and perpetuates negative stereotypes of the African American community.

In the face of criticism, Marsalis has maintained a steadfast position, defending his right to express his views and engage in intellectual discourse about jazz. He views the freedom to critique as essential, refusing to accept a suppression of voices and ideas, which he sees as a step backward.

The debate surrounding Wynton Marsalis encapsulates the complex and dynamic nature of jazz as an art form, where tradition and innovation coexist, and where different artists and critics engage in a passionate dialogue about its past, present, and future.

PERSONAL LIFE

Wynton Marsalis's personal life is deeply intertwined with a rich tapestry of musical heritage and family bonds.

He is the son of the late jazz luminary Ellis Marsalis Jr., a renowned pianist whose contributions to the world of jazz were widely celebrated. The mantle of musical prowess extends further back in his family lineage, as he is the grandson of Ellis Marsalis Sr., a testament to the enduring legacy of musical excellence in the Marsalis clan.

Within his family, the bonds of music run deep and wide. Wynton's older brother, Branford Marsalis, is a celebrated saxophonist whose virtuosity has left an indelible mark on the jazz landscape. His younger brother, Delfeayo Marsalis, not only wields a trombone with mastery but is also a producer, contributing to the creation of musical artistry. Completing this ensemble of musical talent is Jason Marsalis, whose rhythmic prowess as a drummer adds yet another layer to the family's musical legacy.

The Marsalis family's musical talents extend to the next generation as well. Wynton's son, Jasper Armstrong Marsalis, is a music producer who goes by the professional moniker Slauson Malone, carving his path in the world of music production.

In matters of faith and spirituality, Wynton Marsalis was raised in the Catholic tradition, reflecting the diverse tapestry of influences that have shaped his life and artistry. His personal journey, rooted in both music and spirituality, continues to inspire and resonate with audiences worldwide, as he remains a beacon of artistic excellence and familial devotion.

AWARDS AND HONOR

Wynton Marsalis's illustrious career has been adorned with a constellation of awards and honors, each a testament to his exceptional contributions to the world of music and culture:

- In 1983, at the astonishingly young age of 22, Marsalis achieved a remarkable feat. He became the sole musician to clinch Grammy Awards in both the jazz and classical music categories during the same year. This extraordinary accomplishment was a precursor to his continued success in these genres.

- Following the release of his debut album in 1982, Marsalis quickly ascended to the pinnacle of acclaim. He swept the polls in DownBeat magazine, earning titles such as Musician of the Year, Best Trumpeter, and Album of the Year. In 2017, his enduring impact on the world of jazz was further underscored as he was inducted into the prestigious DownBeat Hall of Fame.

- In 1997, Wynton Marsalis etched his name in history by becoming the first jazz musician to receive the Pulitzer Prize for Music. His groundbreaking oratorio, "Blood on the Fields," resonated deeply with audiences and critics alike, earning him this esteemed accolade.

- His contributions to the arts and culture have garnered Marsalis several national honors. He received the National Medal of Arts from President George W. Bush in 2005, and the National Humanities Medal for his profound impact on the cultural landscape.

- Marsalis's enduring influence on jazz led to his designation as an NEA Jazz Master, a recognition of his pivotal role in preserving and advancing the art form.

- His global reach and musical prowess are evident in his extensive touring history. He has performed in approximately 30 countries and on every continent, except Antarctica, captivating audiences worldwide with his virtuosity.

- Marsalis has been recognized by numerous organizations and institutions, receiving accolades such as the Louis Armstrong Memorial Medal, the Algur H. Meadows Award for Excellence in the Arts, and induction into the American Academy of Achievement. The I Have a Dream Foundation dubbed him an Honorary Dreamer, celebrating his commitment to education and inspiration.

- International recognition includes the Dutch Edison Award, the French Grand Prix du Disque, and the city of Vitoria, Spain, awarding him their esteemed gold medal. The Royal Academy of Music in Britain bestowed upon him the honor of honorary membership, the highest distinction for a non-British citizen.

- The city of Marciac, France, paid tribute to his pivotal role in their annual jazz festival by erecting a bronze statue in his honor. The French Ministry of Culture recognized his contributions by bestowing upon him the rank of Knight in the Order of Arts and Literature.

- France, in particular, holds Marsalis in high esteem. In 2008, he was awarded France's highest distinction, the insignia of Chevalier of the Legion of Honour, acknowledging his profound impact on the nation's cultural heritage.

- Marsalis has been conferred honorary degrees from numerous esteemed institutions, including the Frost School of Music at the University of Miami, the University of Scranton, Kenyon College, New York University, Columbia University, Connecticut

College, Harvard University, Howard University, Northwestern University, Princeton University, the University of Vermont, the State University of New York, and the University of Michigan.

Wynton Marsalis's life and career have been punctuated by these accolades and honors, a reflection of his enduring commitment to the world of music and his unwavering dedication to the enrichment of culture and the arts.

DISCOGRAPHY

Wynton Marsalis's exceptional talent and contributions to the world of jazz have been recognized and celebrated through a series of prestigious awards and accolades, particularly in the realm of jazz and instrumental performance:

Best Jazz Instrumental Solo:
- "Think of One" (1983)
- "Hot House Flowers" (1984)
- "Black Codes (From the Underground)" (1985)

Best Jazz Instrumental Album, Individual or Group:
- "Black Codes (From the Underground)" (1985)
- "J Mood" (1986)
- "Marsalis Standard Time, Vol. I" (1987)

Best Instrumental Soloist(s) Performance (with orchestra):

- Raymond Leppard (conductor), Wynton Marsalis, and the National Philharmonic Orchestra for "Haydn: Trumpet Concerto in E Flat/Leopold Mozart: Trumpet Concerto in D/Hummel: Trumpet Concerto in E Flat" (1983)
- Raymond Leppard (conductor), Wynton Marsalis, and the English Chamber Orchestra for "Wynton Marsalis, Edita Gruberova: Handel, Purcell, Torelli, Fasch, Molter" (1984)

These awards reflect Marsalis's exceptional skill as a trumpeter and his significant contributions to the jazz and instrumental music genres. His remarkable talent has left an indelible mark on the world of music, and these accolades stand as a testament to his enduring impact.

IMPACT AND LEGACY

Wynton Marsalis is a musical virtuoso whose influence and impact on the world of music, particularly jazz, extend far beyond his remarkable talent as a trumpeter, composer, and bandleader. His contributions have transcended the boundaries of genres and generations, leaving an indelible mark on the cultural and educational landscape.

Perhaps the most significant aspect of Wynton Marsalis's influence is his unwavering commitment to preserving the traditions of jazz. At a time when the genre was evolving rapidly, Marsalis championed the roots of jazz, emphasizing the importance of blues, standards, and swing. His dedication to these fundamental elements helped rekindle interest in traditional jazz and introduced it to a new generation of listeners.

Marsalis's impact on music education is immeasurable. He has been a tireless advocate for music education and has worked extensively to bring jazz into classrooms around the world. As the director of the Juilliard Jazz Studies program, he has mentored and nurtured young talents, ensuring that the legacy of jazz is passed onto future generations.

While dedicated to tradition, Marsalis is not bound by it. He has been a pioneer in pushing the boundaries of jazz, collaborating with musicians from diverse genres and experimenting with new forms. His ability to bridge the gap between classical and jazz music is a testament to his versatility and innovation.

Wynton Marsalis's numerous Grammy Awards, Pulitzer Prize for Music, and other accolades not only acknowledge his personal achievements but also shine a spotlight on the significance of jazz as an art form. His recognition has elevated jazz to a level of prominence and respect it deserves.

Marsalis's role as a cultural ambassador cannot be overstated. His tireless efforts to promote jazz and American culture worldwide have fostered a global appreciation for this quintessentially American art form. He has toured extensively, performing on nearly every continent and sharing the magic of jazz with diverse audiences.

Beyond music, Marsalis has used his platform to engage in social commentary. His outspoken views on issues such as hip-hop and culture have sparked discussions and encouraged critical thinking. He challenges stereotypes and encourages dialogue on important societal issues.

Marsalis's journey from a young trumpet prodigy to a global icon serves as an inspiration to aspiring musicians. His dedication, discipline, and commitment to excellence are qualities that resonate with anyone pursuing a passion.

In sum, Wynton Marsalis's influence and impact on music, culture, and education are immeasurable. He has played a pivotal role in preserving jazz traditions, expanding its horizons, and passing on the torch to future generations. His contributions have elevated jazz to new heights and ensured its enduring relevance in a rapidly changing world.

Printed in Great Britain
by Amazon